# East vs. West

# East vs. West

## Ralph Schoenstein
## and
## Arnold Roth

Published by Simon & Schuster
New York

Copyright © 1981 by Ralph Schoenstein and Arnold Roth
All rights reserved
including the right of reproduction
in whole or in part in any form
Published by Wallaby Books
A Simon & Schuster Division of
Gulf & Western Corporation
Simon & Schuster Building
1230 Avenue of the Americas
New York, New York 10020

WALLABY and colophon are trademarks
of Simon & Schuster

First Wallaby Books Printing September 1981
10 9 8 7 6 5 4 3 2 1
Manufactured in the United States of America

Library of Congress Catalog Card Number: 81–50911

ISBN 0–671–43047–5

Book design by H. Roberts Design

*To New York's finest, Charles and Adam*
            *and*
*To California's gold, Bill Murray and Jules Greenberg*
            *and*
*To Lori, a cosmic joy*

# Preface

*East is East*
*And West is West*
*And St. Louis is the pits*

These wingèd lines, which have been traced to either Carl Sandburg or the wall of a Shell station in Detroit, tell us volumes or perhaps almost nothing about the difference between East and West, a difference so mystical that neither this book nor an intelligible one could possibly capture it. But it is better to try and fail than to never fail at all.

"You cannot ever hope to understand the East," Pearl Buck once told me.

"The east of what?" I replied, and her interest in our dialogue seemed to disappear.

In spite of her denseness, however, the word "east" is clearly relative, for East Orange is certainly west of an awful lot, and below even more.

To make things even more accessible for busy readers on the go, on the make, and on the pill, this book uses only generalizations; and I am sorry that some of my favorites, such as *All Swedes are despondent*, *All dentists are strange*, and *There are never any Jewish catchers in the National*

*League*, could not have been included, but there is already too much irrelevant material in the book.

Arnold Roth's drawings are also in, filling space that could have been used for telephone numbers; but the publisher insisted that these drawings, originally done for subway cars, be included for readers who cannot understand the text. One such reader is Roth, for his art does not illuminate the text so much as interrupt it.

"It is not interrupted enough," I can hear Pearl Buck saying now.

*Ralph Schoenstein*

# East vs. West

To a Californian, New Yorkers give nothing to charity because they count on being mugged at least once a month. The streets of New York are about as safe as the streets of Danang used to be, but not as clean.

To a New Yorker, every Californian drives a Rolls-Royce, a Mercedes, or a truck full of Mexicans.

**The map of New York City, as imagined by a Californian.**

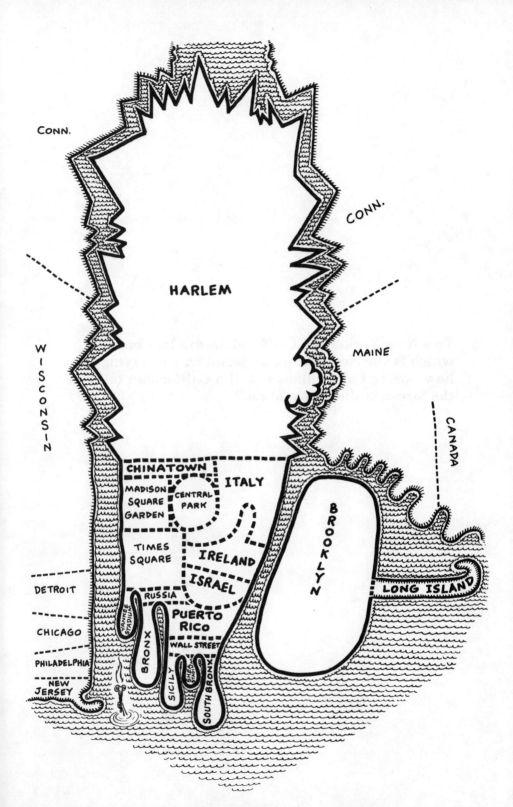

To a New Yorker, all Californians are laid back, which is the New Yorker's special way of saying how boring Californians are. If a Californian talks in the forest, is there any sound?

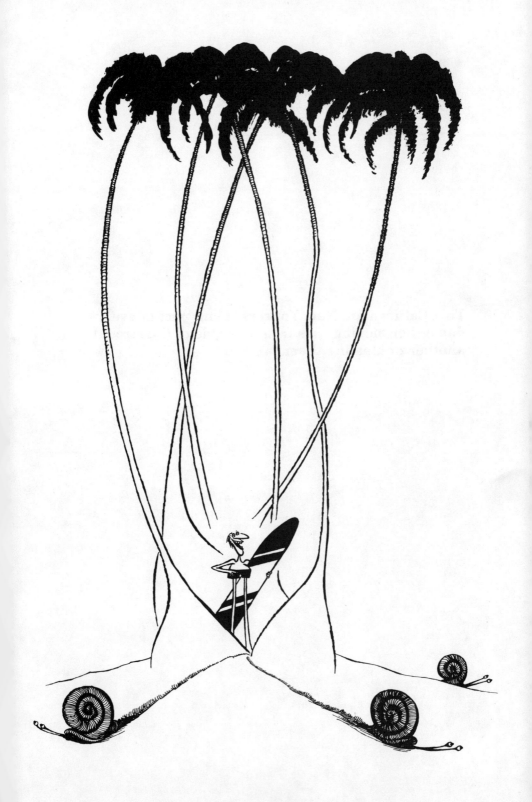

To a Californian, New Yorkers spend part of every day either moving cars from one side of the street to another or stealing them.

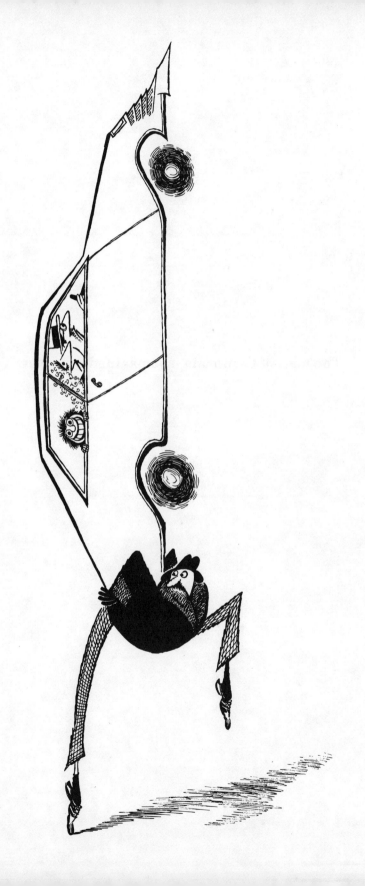

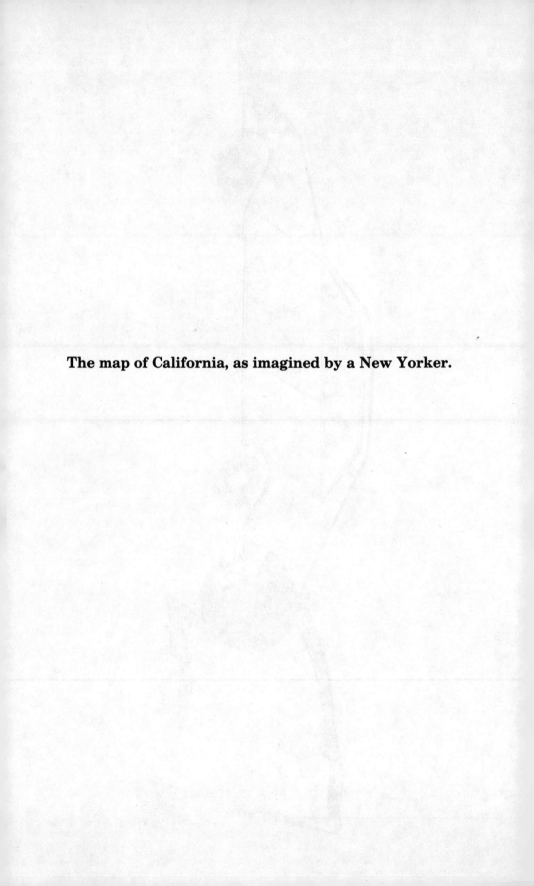

The map of California, as imagined by a New Yorker.

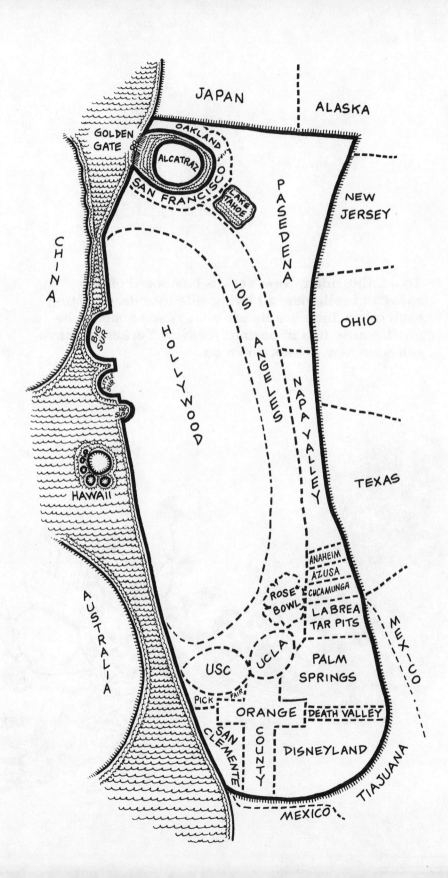

To a Californian, New York is composed of many races and religions, all living side by side, detesting each other. Immigrants are always welcome in the city because it is important for New Yorkers to have someone new to look down on.

To a New Yorker, Californians weigh less than other people because of their frequent face peels. In fact, there are now more faces than oranges peeled in California.

To a Californian, eighty-two percent of New York is covered by graffiti, but unfortunately some of the city still shows through.

A California mugging, as envisioned by a New Yorker.

To a Californian, New York is ninety-three percent prostitutes, pushers, pimps and other undesirables. Every third person in New York should be arrested, even the cops.

To a New Yorker, a Californian will not make a move
without consulting a horoscope, which she often
uses to tell her the best time to consult a horoscope.

To a Californian, the air in New York is fit to breathe only if you have a poison-gas deficiency.

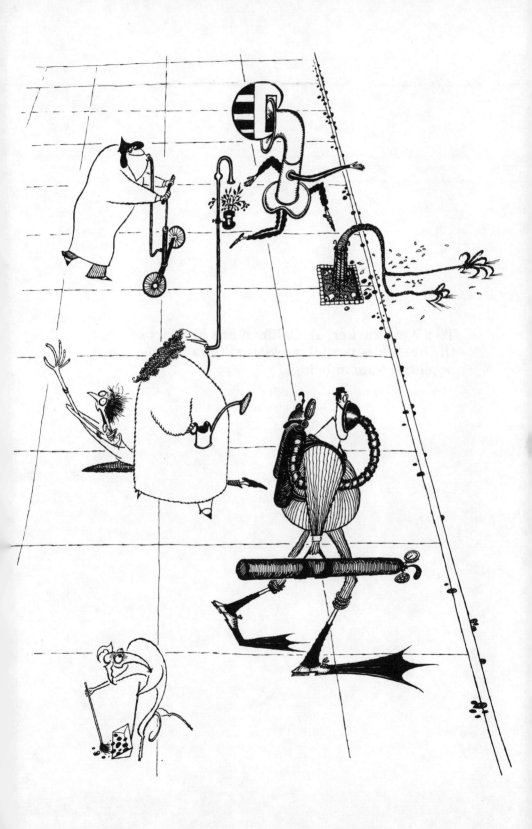

To a New Yorker, all Californians are part of
the human potential movement because they are
potential human beings.

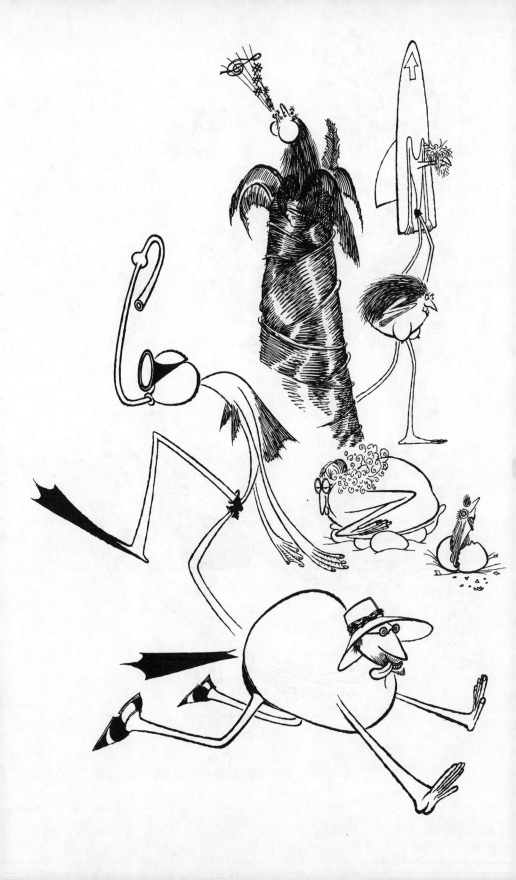

To a Californian, all New Yorkers are on the brink, the fringe, or the edge. It is hard to tell when a New Yorker is having a nervous breakdown because he keeps acting like everyone else.

To a New Yorker, the last sincere remark in California was made by Balboa, who took a look at the Pacific and said, "I guess it's okay if you like the beach, but I wanted to go to the mountains this year."

To a Californian, everyone in New York is on welfare or would like to be. There are more sponges in New York than in the waters off Greece.

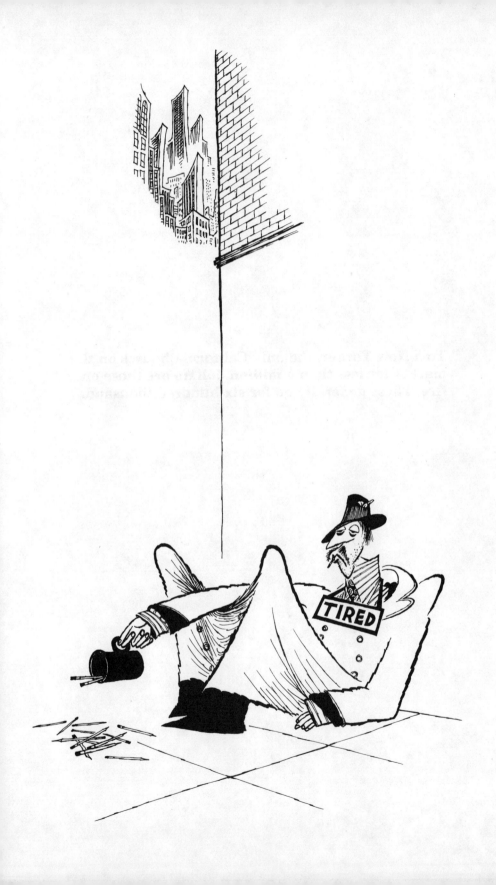

To a New Yorker, the only California houses on the market for less than a million dollars are those on fire. These generally go for six hundred thousand.

To a Californian, a person must prove himself criminally insane before he is allowed to drive a taxi in New York. For New York cabbies, honesty and stopping at red lights are both optional.

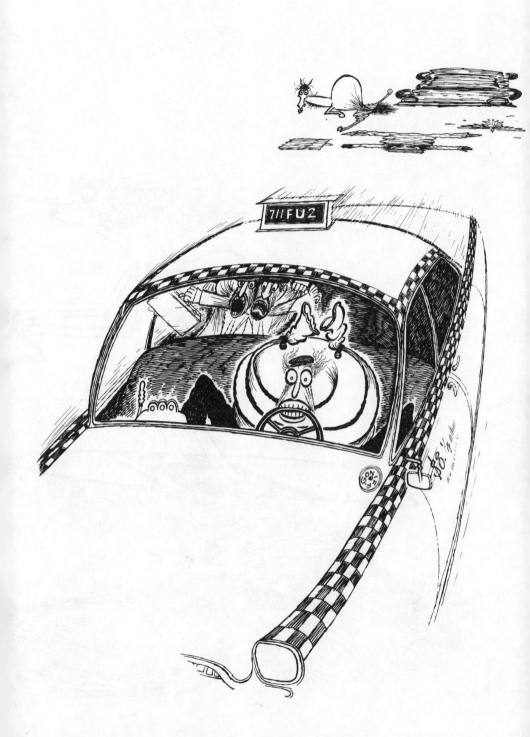

To a New Yorker, Californians never walk anywhere because walking is illegal in some neighborhoods and embarrassing in others. There are only four shoe-repair shops in the entire state (three of which take only clogs) because many Californians have never learned to walk at all. They learn how to surf at the age of two and soon afterward learn how to drive.

To a Californian, New York is owned by (A) real-estate magnates and (B) roaches, both of whom have similar personalities.

To a New Yorker, Californians spend more time at the beach than sand crabs do, and while there, they are always doing handstands, having sex, and brushing their teeth. In fact, some Californians are born on the beach, usually during low tide, and go to school there, majoring in tanning. A tan is more important to a Californian than his wife and children—unless, of course, they have gone out for more lotion.

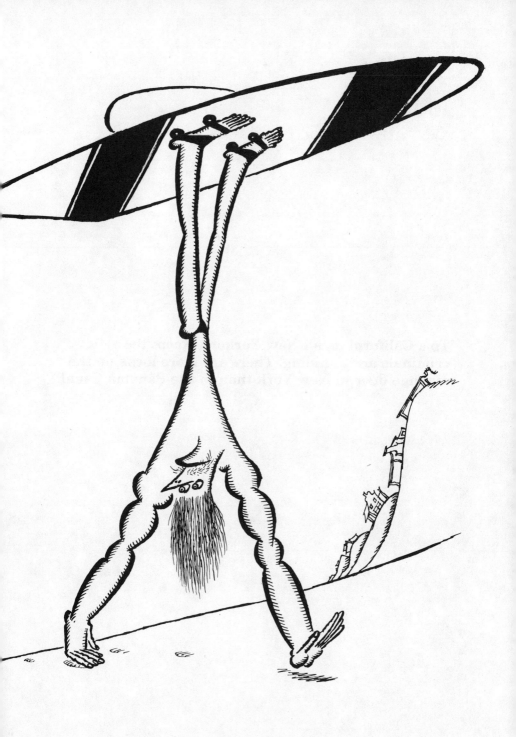

To a Californian, all New Yorkers except the criminals are in hiding. There are more locks on the average door in New York than in the Panama Canal.

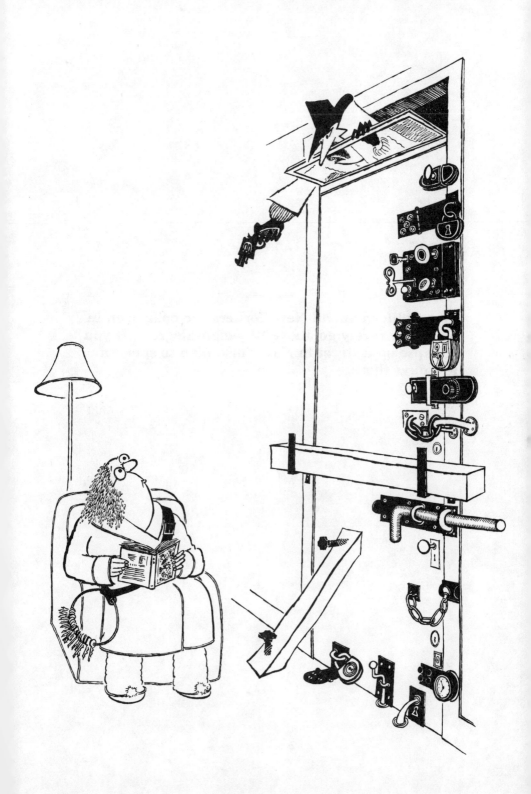

To a Californian, all New Yorkers are cold; even in heat they rarely go above fifty-eight degrees. If you collapse on a street in New York, plan to spend a few days there.

To a New Yorker, all Californians belong to strange religious cults, none of which observe Yom Kippur. If you find a Californian wandering in the hills dressed only in a sheet, he is not in a pledge class of the Klan. Eighty-three percent of the world's religious fanatics are Californians. In fact, it is now believed that both Buddha and Mohammed came from Mendocino.

**A Californian's idea of New York palm trees.**

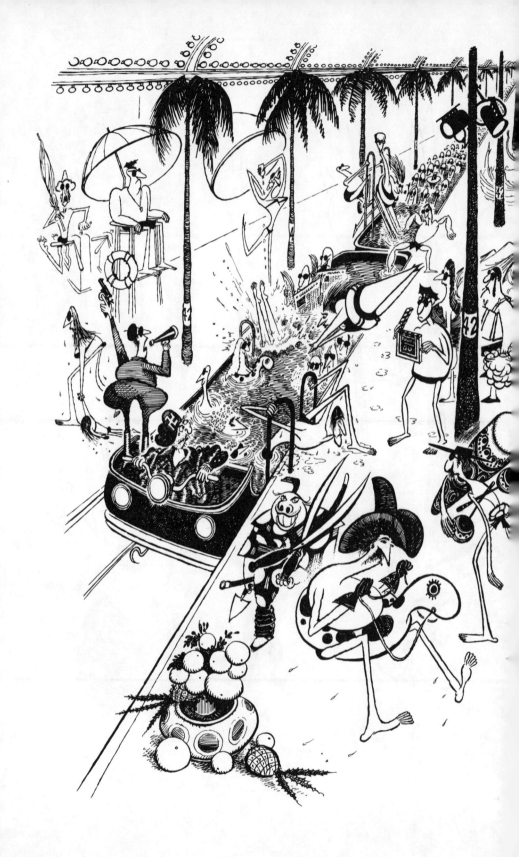

**A New Yorker's concept of the Los Angeles subway.**

To a Californian, the basic difference between the people and the pigeons in New York is that the pigeons don't shit on each other.

To a New Yorker, on September 4, 1981, Los Angeles celebrated its bicentennial: two hundred years of people trying to find it.

Rub-a-dub-dub,
Three Californians in a tub.
The butcher, the baker, the Los Angeles Laker.

To a New Yorker, Californians tend to act crazy when the Santa Ana wind blows, and also when it doesn't.

To a Californian, a New York doorman is a uniformed drunk who carries your bundles at Christmastime.

To a New Yorker, everyone in California is a faddist and is always into something new, like mind control or somebody's wife. The only fad that has never caught on in California is civilization.

To a New Yorker, Californians don't *know* anything, possibly because the only things they read are freeway signs, surfboard ads, and the labels of skin creams. If you have a conversation with a Californian, never refer to anything that took place before this morning. The only entrance requirement for a California college is a knowledge of its zip code.

To a Californian, all New York is looney tunes: on every street some looney is attacking you with tunes. The radios in New York are now bigger than most of the apartments.

To a New Yorker, all Californians are blond, even the blacks. There are, in fact, whole neighborhoods that are zoned only for blond people. The only way to tell the difference between California and Sweden is that the Swedes speak better English.

To a Californian, the boys in New York who used to play stickball are now playing stick-up. Today's city children seem not to mind taking their allowances from strangers.

To a New Yorker, there are earthquakes every few days in California, but they are never reported unless an Elizabeth Arden's disappears. Californians are very sensitive about the way that the state will not hold still. In fact, they are now putting out the story that the San Andreas Fault is a missed first serve in the San Andreas Open.

To a Californian, you could lubricate a fleet of
DC 10s with the grease from the food served every
day at lunch counters in New York.

To a New Yorker, almost everything in California is now drive-in. There are even drive-in whorehouses, some of which are called film studios.

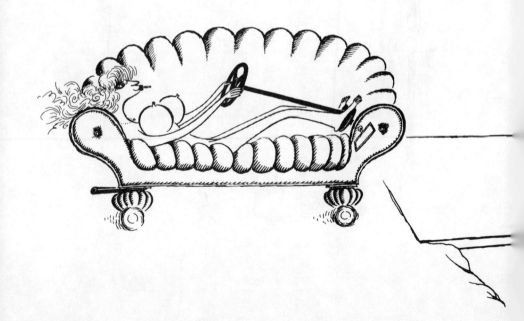

To a Californian, there is more fleecing in New York
than in Australia. If you ask a New Yorker for
the right time, he will give you some other time,
possibly a quarter to four.

To a New Yorker, California politics are slightly less stable than politics in El Salvador. The problem is that Californians can never remember if they are Republicans or Democrats, and so they spend a lot of time guessing. Any state that can elect both Ronald Reagan and Jerry Brown is now ready to elect Fats Domino. Proposition 13 originated in California because most of the people thought it was a new cologne.